SCOTTISH HIGHLANDS SERIES

FORT WILLIAM & OBAN

David O'Neil

ARGYLL ✦ PUBLISHING

© Text and photos David O'Neil 2007
© Map on pps 4/5 Collins Bartholomew Ltd 2007
Reproduced by Permission of HarperCollins Publishers
www.collinsbartholomew.com

First published in 2007 by
Argyll Publishing
Glendaruel
Argyll PA22 3AE
Scotland
www.argyllpublishing.com

The author has asserted his moral rights.

**British Library Cataloguing-in-Publication Data.
A catalogue record for this book is available
from the British Library.**

ISBN 978 1 906134 00 6

Printing: Thomson Litho, Glasgow

Contents

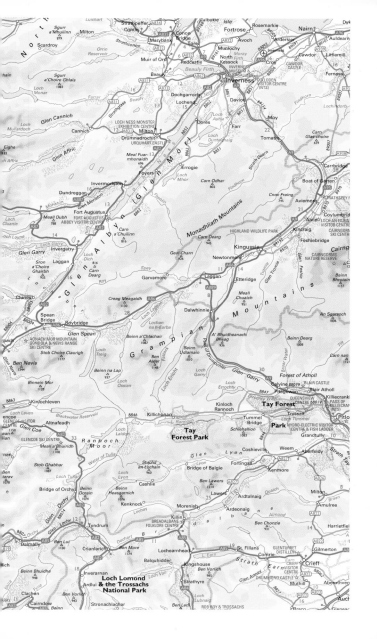

Preface

This book is not a history book, nor is it a definitive guide to the region. It is designed to encourage the reader to seek out for his or herself the beauty of the country and the fascinating history of its people. I have suggested with words and pictures, where to look. It's up to the reader to fill in the gaps. There is no excuse for the belief that this area is for climbers and walkers only. As a touring centre it's second to none. Turn the page and start your journey.

THE TOWN of **Fort William** has a wide range of activities to offer. Apart from the obvious walking and climbing, there are facilities for the less energetic. In the centre is the Tourist Office, located in Cameron Square, next to the West Highland Museum. Leaflets from the Tourist Office indicate some of the other things to be done. 'Treasures of the Earth', just outside town in **Corpach**, boat trips to Seal Island in Loch Linnhe start from the Crannog Pier.

On the Inverness Road, at the junction with the Mallaig road, can be found the **Ben Nevis distillery**. Dating from 1825, this was the home of 'Long John' whisky, named for the founder, John MacDonald, who was 6 ft 5in tall.

On the Inverness road, past the Ben Nevis Hotel, is a signposted road to **Inverlochy Castle**. The Castle, now a ruin, was built in 1275 by Sir John (The Black) Comyn. The Castle, based on the round Comyn Tower was the scene of important events, the most famous being the Battle of Inverlochy in 1645, where the Marquis of Montrose defeated an army twice the size, composed of Covenanters. Montrose's Royalists, marched from Loch Ness, through the snow, to achieve this famous victory.

At Aonach Mor the **ski lift** rises 2300 ft to the Snow Goose restaurant, open all the year round. The Caledonian Canal is at **Banavie** just one mile from Corpach at the end of the Canal where 'Treasures of the Earth' is located, and of course during the summer, on the famous West Highland Line to **Mallaig**, the 'Jacobite' steam train runs daily.

The town of Fort William owes its existence to the fort built in 1650, following parliamentary rule under Oliver Cromwell. General Monk built the first fort at its present site. This was replaced by the more elaborate building in 1690-1 under William of Orange. The ruins still exist on the shores of Loch Linnhe.

There are many places of interest, for the artist, the historian and the photographer. For those who like to just point the car and drive, there is a wonderful array of destinations suggested in the following pages.

Fort William
Tourist Office 01397 703781
Crannog Cruises 01397 700714
Ski Lift 01397 705825
Ben Nevis Distillery 01397 700200
West Highland Museum 01397 702169
Treasures of the Earth 01397 772283

Ben Nevis

THE HIGHEST mountain in Britain, **Ben Nevis** dominates the skyline above Fort William. Part of the Grampian Mountains, all three peaks in the Nevis range are over 4000 ft. The whole area has been a Mecca for climbers for the last two hundred years.

The summit of the Ben is accessible and the footpath, called the pony track, is a popular walk with summer visitors. It has never been easy. About 4 hours up and 3.5 hours down, the path was created in the latter years of the nineteenth century, because of the establishment of the Meteorological Observatory that was built there in the 1880s. The Observatory operated until the early 1900s, supplying data on the weather via telegraph throughout the twenty years of its existence. A hotel was built next to the Observatory, the guests being conveyed by pony/pony cart to the summit. The track is the path still used by walkers today.

Climbers normally shun the path and gain access to the summit either further up Glen Nevis, or by other routes around the mountain base. Access to the pony track is from **Glen Nevis Centre**, or opposite the **Youth Hostel**, both on the road up the glen.

The glen itself is one of the most beautiful, scenically in the Highlands and the road from Fort William can be followed up to the upper falls. It is possible to walk the river banks within this area, surrounded by the flanks of the mountains on both sides. The River Nevis runs through the Glen. The lower falls, seen on the way up can be examined more closely if you use the car park near the bridge over the river. Called 'Poldhu', meaning the Black Pool, the waters, tumble into a pool said to be 15 feet deep.

Further down the glen, there is normally a herd of Highland Cattle grazing. They are fairly docile and visitor friendly, but if there are calves about remember mothers can be quite protective, sometimes aggressively so. Be warned!

Dipper

Ben Nevis
Scottish Youth Hostel 01397 700436
Glen Nevis Chalets &Caravans
                01397 702191
Nevis Centre 01397 705922
Glen Nevis Restaurant 01397 705459
Ben Nevis Inn 01397701227

Cia-Aig Falls

LEAVE Fort William on the Inverness road. One mile past **Spean Bridge**, at the top of the hill by the Commando Memorial, there is a road leading across the glen to Gairlochy, on the Caledonian Canal. On the far bank the road forks, left to Banavie, right to **Achnacarry**, the Estate of Cameron of Lochiel.

The road winds through thick woodlands past the shores of Loch Lochy. From there it runs past the cottage where the Camerons lived during World War II, whilst the estate was used by the War Office for training Commandos. Beyond the cottage along a glen known as the Dark Mile, the road leads to **Loch Arkaig**.

However before reaching the loch side, you pass over the Clunie Bridge on the River Arkaig. On the right is

Commando Memorial

the double waterfall where Bonnie Prince Charlie is reputed to have hidden from the Redcoats, the Cia-Aig falls.

Below the falls is the Witch's Pool, the name comes from a story told about young Clunie, in the eighteenth century. He decided to build the bridge to replace the ford, in use at that time. He commenced the building but fell ill and was expected to die, with the bridge half built. From nowhere a lady named Morag appeared and cured the young man's sickness. She then disappeared and was last seen entering the pool, and became known as the witch of the pool. Why should she have bothered curing Young Clunie? Local lore suggests that the bridge replacing the ford, would allow the witch to rest in peace thereafter.

Clan Cameron Museum 01397 712090

Commando Memorial

STANDING outlined against the sky on the hilltop beyond the village of Spean Bridge, the Memorial stands on the left side of the road. Three soldiers, in World War II uniform, are represented in accurate detail down to the studs on their boots. These figures which are eight feet tall are a reminder that during World War II this whole area was a training ground. The memorial stands on the opposite side of the glen from the wartime base on the estate of Cameron of Lochiel at Achnacarry. Here for three months, the men went through the most rigorous training devised at that time. The plaque states that the three men look over their training ground; however the monument faces the other way. The sculptor intended they should overlook Achnacarry. The commando committee decided that no self-respecting commando would ever want to see Achnacarry again, so they turned the statues. The **Cameron Museum** has a section devoted to the history of the commando presence in the area. There is also a Commando exhibition at the **Spean Bridge Hotel**.

At Spean Bridge can be found a woollen mill, part of the Edinburgh Woollen Mill Group, a Post Office and a mini-market, and a Tourist Office.

Spean Bridge Woollen Mill 01397 712260
Tourist Office 01397 712576
Commando Exhibition (Hotel) 01397 712250

Fort Augustus

THE TOWN of **Fort Augustus** stands at the foot of Loch Ness. The Fort, constructed by General Wade between 1728-1742, was named for William Augustus, Duke of Cumberland who was Commander of the forces of his brother George I. Built on the shores of **Loch Ness** it was a bastion of the King's rule in Scotland. It was captured briefly by the Jacobite forces but swiftly returned to Royal occupation and survived as a fort until the late eighteenth century, when it was handed over to Lord Lovat, on whose land it stood. He in turn passed it on to a sect of Benedictine monks, who turned it into a monastery. This survived until the end of the twentieth century. It is now being converted to apartments.

The **Caledonian Canal** enters Loch Ness at this point. The set of four locks make an interesting feature; the main road crosses the canal by Swing Bridge. Beside the bridge is the quay for Loch Cruises, and the Clansman

Exhibition provides an insight into Highland life in the eighteenth century.

There are several places to eat in the village and a rare breed's park. Relics of the abandoned Invergarry–Fort Augustus Railway can be seen in the River Oich that runs parallel to the canal. The pillars of the old Rail Bridge still stand. Formerly known as Kilchumin, the town was the home of John Anderson, carpenter friend of Robert Burns, and maker of his coffin, immortalised in the song, 'John Anderson my Jo John'.

An interesting feature of the village is the Woollen Mill shop that stands beside the canal. A former 'mail order' church, complete with belfry, dates from 1909. Not bad for a tin hut!

Clansman Centre 01320 366444
Tourist Office 01320 366367
Cruise Loch Ness 01320 366221

Castle Urquhart

THERE has been legend of castles built on this spot from time immemorial. In the stories of ancient battles within the area the castle or its earlier versions have always figured.

The fortunes of the early Kings, the battles of the Lord of the Isles, all include references to **Urquhart Castle**. It has been sacked and rebuilt many times in its highly chequered career. By the seventeenth century the Grants had managed to reconstruct the castle to produce the basis for the present picturesque ruins. The structure was refurbished once more by the soldiers of Cromwell's army, but in 1689 the garrison of Whig soldiers blew the castle up, to prevent its use by any other troops. The Laird of Grant was paid a huge amount of money in compensation but the castle was never restored.

In the past the loch level was lower, the level rose 6ft when the Caledonian Canal was opened. Urquhart Castle is the southern terminus for the 'Jacobite Queen' which sails regularly from Inverness. This popular trip is a guided tour of the upper loch and the Canal; tickets are often combined with castle entry.

Drumnadrochit, just up the glen from the Castle, is the home of the Loch Ness Exhibition, and as a tourist centre, to alternative cruises, craft shops, cafés and restaurants. There is a tourist information centre and toilets in the car park.

Castle Urquhart 01456 450551
Jacobite Cruises 01463 233999
Loch Ness Exhibition 01456 450573

The Canal Basin, Banavie

ON THE A830 the Basin lies at the top of **Neptune's Staircase**. Turn right immediately past the Canal Bridge, the car park is on the right. Access to the canal bank is from the car park. The basin is at the top of the set of locks. This anchorage on the Caledonian Canal is the winter home of many of the boats that ply the canal during the summer season. From this location can be seen the whole sweep of the Nevis Range, dominated by Ben Nevis.

From here walkers can follow the towpath north to Gairlochy, Loch Lochy, Loch Oich and Loch Ness. Inverness lies at the other end of the canal; the footpath follows the right side of the Canal north and is part of the newly established **Great Glen Way**. In the other direction the famous Neptune's Staircase stretches down to the Mallaig Road, and the end of the canal at Corpach. The eight locks form a magnificent foreground to the vista of Loch Linnhe, stretching southwards to Mull and the Atlantic Ocean. The building of the canal was commenced by Thomas Telford in 1804 and completed in 1824, taking twice as long as anticipated. The fact that it cost twice as much as the estimate will come as no surprise. The cost? One million pounds, and despite the extended time for construction, the canal had to be closed for nine years in 1834, to replace the inferior materials used by the contractors in the building of the many locks. There was a steamer service between Banavie and Muirtown Locks, Inverness, in 1823, this ran daily in both directions until the 1930s when one of the ships burned to the waterline. The remaining ship continued in service for some years on its own, the trip becoming spread over a two day period. It is possible to walk the short journey down Neptune's Staircase to Corpach. Here the canal meets Loch Linnhe and once again fine views of Ben Nevis can be enjoyed.

Meadowsweet

Glenfinnan

FIFTEEN miles west of Fort William, on the Mallaig road, is the spectacular memorial to the **Jacobite uprising**. It stands between the road and Loch Shiel on the left side. On the right is the equally spectacular railway viaduct, made famous by the recent Harry Potter films, and built by Robert MacAlpine early in the twentieth century. The Monument was completed in the mid eighteenth century, by direction of MacDonald of Glen Alladale. The figure on the top of the column is not Bonnie Prince Charlie, but apparently Glen Alladale's son, whose picture hung next to that of the Prince in Glen Alladale's house.

There is a **National Trust Visitor Centre** which has a detailed history of the Jacobite uprising, which of course ties in with the raising of the Jacobite banner within the glen in 1745. The centre controls access to the top of the Monument for those intrepid people with the energy to climb the stairs. Beside the Centre is a path that climbs the hill behind, and leads to a viewpoint with spectacular views of both viaduct and Loch Shiel. It is well worth the effort, though it can be quite slippery when wet.

The viaduct itself is part of the famous **West Highland Line**. The section from Fort William to Mallaig was built entirely by Robert MacAlpine who used concrete for all the bridges and viaducts. Despite advice and gloomy forecasts condemning his faith in unreinforced concrete, Concrete Bob, as he became known, went ahead and the use of the line to this present day is a tribute to his faith in the material.

The Monument does not indicate the spot where the banner was raised. It is believed that happened on the slopes of the Glen. The Monument was part of a hunting lodge which was demolished leaving the single tower standing. Significantly the tower is inclined to lean to one side or the other because of the instability of the underlying peaty soil.

Leaving the visitor centre towards Mallaig, on the left is St Finnan's church. You may notice the bell is in a shelter on the grass in front of the church. This is because the bell turned out to be too big and heavy for the bell loft. It has been on the lawn since it arrived. There is a sign above the bell inviting people to 'Ring me and pray'.

The railway station contains a little museum and has both a restaurant car and a sleeper available for use.

National Trust Glenfinnan 01397 722250
Loch Shiel Cruises 01687 470322
Glenfinnan Dining Car & Sleeper 01397 722300

Scots Pine – Loch Eilt

FOLLOWING the railway line towards Mallaig, the road from Glenfinnan passes down through three glens to **Loch Eilt** (Loch of the Hind). This freshwater loch is popular with fishermen, though only with permission of the owners. There are several islands in the loch and it can be clearly seen that the islands have heavy wood cover. Legend has it that the prevalence of Scots Pine trees on the islands date from the aftermath of the Jacobite uprising.

No memorial was permitted for the Jacobite dead, who were regarded as traitors by the government. The local families decided to remember their dead by planting a pine tree for each of their lost kin. This would be the third generation of pines since Culloden, the trees left to re-seed themselves more or less successfully.

Below Loch Eilt lies a Lochan (little loch) The island in this loch is also covered with Scots Pine and is believed to be a similar memorial.

Loch Nan Uamh

LOCH NAN UAMH is where Bonnie Prince Charlie first landed on the Scottish mainland. It was also his final departure point, after the Battle of Culloden. Details of these events can be found at the visitor centre, Glenfinnan.

The viaduct illustrated in the picture has its own legend. Part of the famous West Highland Line on the route to Mallaig, this viaduct was the scene of a tragedy that occurred during the construction. A horse and cart, loaded with stone reversed to the edge of one of the columns, it reversed too far and fell into the concrete and stone filled 'form' causing the horse to break a leg when it fell. The weight was too great to be recovered, so the horse was put down on the spot and the concrete continued to be poured. X-rays show the skeleton of the horse and cart, still within the broad pillar.

The name is Gaelic for the loch of the caves, and caves can be found on the right of the road as it passes the shore beyond the viaduct. There is also a cairn, which claims to mark where Charles last set foot on his ancestral homeland.

To the south, across the water can be seen the Ardna-murchan Peninsula, the most westerly point on the mainland of Britain. The magnificent forest all around this area is mainly of oak trees, and has been untouched for hundreds of years.

Mallaig and Arisaig

AT THE END of Concrete Bob's famous rail line is the town of **Mallaig**. Ferry port and fishing centre, this is the point of departure for Armadale on the Isle of Skye, and the small isles of Rhum Eigg and Muck. The fishing fleet that still operates has been much reduced over the years owing to the reduction of fish stocks, and the inhibitions imposed by the European Union. The harbour is still a busy place, seals tout for fish and small boats vie for room with the ferries and commercial craft.

The town plays host to the influx of tourists brought daily during the summer, by coach, and the 'Jacobite' steam train. Many of the coaches are en route to Skye, others on excursion from Fort William. There are ample facilities for feeding the incomers ranging from the Fishermen's Mission to the various hotels and restaurants through the town. The Mallaig Marine World and the Heritage Centre provide additional diversion, especially when it's wet.

En Route to Mallaig, **Arisaig** is a village on the shore opposite the island of Eigg. Also a one-time fishing port, this is now a leisure spot, popular with coastal cruising yachts that call in and use the harbour as a centre for sailing in the Minch. The Old Library Restaurant and the Arisaig Hotel provide food within the village. The village boasts a serious bookshop and a chandlery. There is also a small boat ferry to Eigg.

Between Arisaig and Mallaig, lie the famous **Silver Sands of Morar**, immortalised in the movie 'Local Hero'. The road runs alongside the beach which is easily accessible. A short diversion just before the bridge will take you along the half mile length of the River Morar to Loch Morar, the deepest loch in Britain, home to 'Morag', sister to Nessie? Over 1000ft deep Loch Morar is popular for fishing and sailing. It has an almost private feel, no shops, no other facilities, just houses and peace. Views of Rhum, Muck and Eigg can be seen all along the coastline.

Old Library, Arisaig 01687 450681
Arisaig Hotel 01687 450210
Arisaig Marine Centre 01687 450224
Mallaig Marine World 01687 462292
Mallaig Heritage Centre 01687 462085
Fishermans Mission 01687 462086

Loch Linnhe

DRIVING down the shores of Loch Linnhe you come to **Nether Lochaber**. Here the loch narrows and the village of Ardgour can be seen on the other side. This point is the end of what was once called Loch Aber (where waters meet). The waters between the narrows and Fort William prior to 1900 were known by that name. Loch Linnhe was the stretch from the narrows south to the Sound of Mull. The narrows were where the cattle were swum across on their way to the markets in the Lowlands. At slack water the distance is less than 400 yards. When the tide is running the waters flow through at several knots, and when the wind blows over the tide, it can cause the ferry over the narrows to stop running.

The village of **Ardgour** has one of the many churches built by Thomas Telford, during the construction of the Caledonian Canal. It is unique, for it has a vestry, not normally found in a Church of Scotland. Ministers do not wear vestments. There was no incumbent for the Ardgour parish, thus the minister had to row over weekly from Onich, requiring somewhere to change from his oilskins, hence the vestry.

Heron

The lighthouse is a Stevenson light, built by the father and uncle of Robert Louis Stevenson. It is said that whilst visiting the building site during the construction, Robert learned the story of the Appin murder and used it in his book *Kidnapped*.

Loch Leven

Goldfinch

Loch Leven

OF ALL the unsung beauty spots in Scotland **Loch Leven** must rate as one of the best. This great slash in the hills between Glencoe and the Mamore hills hides the tidal waters of Loch Leven flowing in from Loch Linnhe. In the days of the **Ballachulish Ferry** the road around Loch Leven was regarded as an inconvenience to say the least. Because the ferry stopped running at dusk, the extra journey round the loch, was regarded as a great trial. When the bridge was built the road was more or less forgotten.

With tourism becoming more popular the road gained a new lease of life, and it is enjoyed for the beauty of its scenery. From Glencoe the road is known as the high road, as it winds up high on the side of the glen. This section was built by German POWs. The lower road on the other side of the loch is visible for most of the length of the high road. Our picture is from the high road looking up the loch towards **Kinlochleven**, the village at the head of the loch. Kinlochleven owes its existence to the Hydro Electric Scheme introduced in 1900. The power station was built to allow the smelting of aluminum. The land bought from Mr Bibby, of shipping fame, was only settled when the smelter was built. Mr Bibby took the Lodge on the north side of the Glen in part payment for the land, and it was at the house, Mamore Lodge, that he entertained King Edward VII, his deer stalking compatriot.

There are several viewpoints around the glen for photographers and artists. The lower road winds along the north side of the loch through green trees mainly birch and oak, though there are pine groves at the lower end of the loch. As you get towards the main Fort William road, you will see the fish farm on the loch side and on the other side of the loch a view of Glencoe and Eilean Munde (The Burial Island of the MacDonalds of Glencoe). The great defunct slate quarries and the village of Ballachulish stand out against the green hills.

Three Sisters, Glencoe

Mamore Lodge Hotel 01855 831213
Kinlochleven Library 01855 831663

Glencoe – Three Sisters

THE THREE Sisters of **Glencoe** are probably the best known mountains in the area. Beinn Fhada, Gearr Aonach and Aonach Dubh, stand out on the south side of the Glen facing the jagged line of the Aonach Eagach ridge. Between Beinn Fhada and Gearr Aonach lies the hidden valley, where, it is said, the MacDonalds hid their stolen cattle from the prying eyes of the outraged owners. Up the glen, above the Sisters is the gorge, where the river runs below the road and twists and turns past the falls below the Three Sisters.

Just before the road starts the gradual drop past the viewpoints, there is a little cottage tucked in the corner. Once the home of the mountaineer Hamish MacInnes, it is now one of the homes of Sir Jimmy Saville, Chieftain of the Lochaber Highland Games.

Down the glen below Loch Achtriochtan lies the area where once lived the people who suffered the massacre in 1692. There are many stories told of the event. This is not the place to comment, suffice to say that the houses that once were scattered across the glen, have long gone, only the odd ruin remains to recall that fearful night.

The story can be learned at the Visitor Centre, at the lower end of the Glen, and at the **Glencoe Museum**. The village of Glencoe also has craft shops and restaurants, Craft & Things, Tighphurst and the Carnoch.

Buachaille Etive Mor

STANDING at the joining of Glen Etive and Glencoe, the Massif of **Buachaille Etive Mor** guards the entrance to both Glens. The name means the great herdsman of Glen Etive. This Munro is probably the most climbed mountain in the Glencoe region. Not a hill to be treated lightly, this mountain has cost more people their lives than any other in the region.

From the Three Sisters the road goes along the Glen past Buachaille Etive Beag, a smaller version of Buachaille Etive Mor. At this point the Devils Staircase rises up on the left. A part of the **West Highland Way**, the staircase climbs over from Glencoe to Glen Leven en route to Glen Nevis. This military road was constructed by General Wade's engineers in the early 1700s to enable the soldiers to get more easily to the Highlands, the better to control the turbulent Highlanders. On the right, Alt Na Feadh is one of the access points to Buachaille Etive Mor. Beyond, the road passes the mountain down to the turnoff to Glen Etive.

Alongside the road can be seen signs of the old road that was replaced in 1934 by the present road.

On the other side of **Glen Etive** the White Corries rise up to dominate **Rannoch Moor** at this point. Here the **Glencoe Ski Lift** operates, the entrance being on the right, 200 yards past the entry to the Kings House Hotel. The hotel has been in this place since the eighteenth century, and still caters for tourists and passing folk. There is also a restaurant at the ski lift.

Glencoe
National Trust 01855 811729
Glencoe Museum 01855 811852
Craft &Things 01855 811325
Ski Lift 01855 851226
Kings House Hotel 01855 851259
Carnoch Restaurant 01855 811140

The Road to Oban

Castle Stalker

THE JOURNEY to Oban takes us from Fort William, down Loch Linnhe through Onich and over Ballachulish Bridge. At the far end of the bridge can be seen the memorial to James Stewart, hanged on that spot for the murder of Campbell of Glenure. From here we are in *Kidnapped* country, where the events detailed in Stevenson's book, occurred. On the left heading down the loch we pass the spot where Campbell died.

A little further on we come to The House of Keil, on the loch side. This is where the bones of James Stewart of Appin are buried. The road follows the loch down to Appin. Offshore can be seen the Isle of Shuna, occupied by animals only, and round the bend we come to the view of **Castle Stalker**. There is a viewpoint here, and a café conveniently located for photography. Castle Stalker as its name implies, is a hunting tower built in the fifteenth century, and held by the Stewarts of Appin until the 1740s. The castle has been fully restored during the 1980s and it is now owned by a Stewart family from Surrey.

The road passes down Loch Creran and over the reconstructed railway bridge at the mouth of upper Loch Creran. Through the village of **Barcaldine** the road passes the Sea Life Centre and continues on to Bender-loch. From here we rejoin Loch Linnhe with the view of Mull across the waters to the west. The last stretch is over the Connel Bridge, and into the area of the castle of Dunstaffnage. This is where Flora MacDonald was first detained after the escape of Bonnie Prince Charlie. Oban is just a step away.

Oban

THE TOWN of **Oban** came to prominence during the nineteenth century. The age of steam brought the railways, and steam ferries came into their own. Because of its location Oban was within reach of the day excursion from

Glasgow and it rapidly became a resort. It was also an important centre for ferry services to the Outer Hebrides. The services once established are still operating today, albeit in attenuated form. The regular service to Fort William and Inverness via the canal has been discontinued, but it is still possible to travel to Barra and Uist, Colonsay and Tiree. Harris and Lewis are served by ferries from Skye and Ullapool.

Above Oban stands the famous **MacCaig's tower**, a monument to the family of Councillor MacCaig. Designed after the Coliseum in Rome, the Tower was built as an act of charity, by the unemployed in Oban. Sadly MacCaig did not finish his project as he died during the construction. It has been a landmark for the last hundred years.

Within easy reach of Oban to the south are several interesting places. **Seil Island** off the shore of which lies the Isle of Easdale is famed for its slate. Both islands are accessible via the bridge over the Atlantic, which spans the arm of the sea between Seil and the mainland. Further south can be found a series of standing stones and the historic hill at **Dunadd**. Dunadd is the former seat of the kings of Dalriada and has prior connections with the Druidic priesthood. **Kilmartin**, apart from the stones and a museum, is a good spot for a coffee break.

The road south towards **Lochgilphead** is scenic with beautiful views. At Ardrishaig the Crinan Canal begins its short journey linking the waters of Loch Fyne to the Atlantic Ocean. An alternative way back to Oban is via Inveraray.

North Pier, Oban

Road to Oban
Accommodation The House of Keil 01631 740255
Dunstaffnage Castle (Historic Scotland) 01631 562465

Oban
Hydro Electric Station Cruachan 01866 822618

Lesser Spotted
Woodpecker

Kilchurn Castle

THE CASTLE that stands on the edge of **Loch Awe** was built in 1440 by Sir Colin Campbell of Glenorchy. Although a picturesque ruin, it has had very meagre history. During the Jacobite uprising in 1745 it was offered to the Hanoverian forces for use against the Jacobites. It reverted to Campbell ownership, but was vacated after a turret was blown down during the same storm that destroyed the Tay Rail Bridge in 1879. Access to the castle is only by boat, the old footpath over the railway line having been closed for safety reasons. The boat service is operated from the railway pier behind Loch Awe Hotel. There is a signpost beside the hotel.

Loch Awe is the longest loch in Scotland and is the source of power for the famous **Cruachan power station** located on the north side of the loch, on the Oban road.

There is a visitor centre and tours are provided for visitors. There is also a tea room and toilets.

A fascinating church is to be seen on the Oban road on the left side between the road and the loch. Saint Conan's Church is unlike any other Church of Scotland. Built in the style of just about every period of church history, it incorporates pieces of recovered stone from other churches, from elsewhere in Scotland. The church is open to the public and is well worth a visit.

Inveraray

THE TOWN of Inveraray is very much integrated with **Inveraray Castle**. The castle, seat of the Clan Campbell stands just out of town, off the Glasgow road. The castle can be seen from the grounds, which are open to the public, and from the first bridge on the road north of town. Both bridges are a credit to William and Robert Adam, who designed them and the present town on the shores of Loch Fyne.

The building of the town and castle was the result of events in the seventeenth century. The then Duke decided to rebuild the castle on a different site. The town at the time was in front of the castle, and had to be moved to make way for the new development. The buildings were designed as a 'complimentary whole' neatly arranged on the loch side. The castle – open to the public throughout the tourist season – dates from the same period, though it was not completed until the early nineteenth century.

Inveraray has in addition the Jail building, part of the original design, now open to the public as a museum, complete with courtroom and sound effects.

Opposite the jail is the double church. On one side, services were in Gaelic, in the other, in English. Nowadays the church is only used for services on one side.

The town pier is occupied by a schooner, the *Arctic Penguin* formerly the property of the Irish Lights and Buoys. It came to Inveraray on its retirement. The name is interesting since there are only Antarctic Penguins. There is also a diesel Puffer, the *Eilean Easdale* the last working Puffer on the west coast, also retired. A Bell Tower memorial dominates the town that gives a fine view.

Inveraray
Inveraray Castle 01499 302203
Inveraray Jail 01499 302381
Maritime Heritage Centre 01499 302213
Tourist Office 01499 810254

Ardnamurchan Point

The lighthouse at Ardnamurchan

TURN LEFT at Ardgour on the other side of Corran Ferry and follow your nose. The journey from the ferry passes through Glen Tarbert to **Loch Sunart** (believed to be a corruption of Svenart, from the Norse occupation of the area), a tidal loch that borders the road for most of the way.

The village of **Strontian** lies on the shore of the loch and has a general store and café. Also just over the bridge, the road on the right leads to **Ariundle** and a café, knitwear and visitor centre called Cozyknits, on the edge of the Nature Reserve that extends up the Glen.

Formerly a mining village, Strontian is the site where Strontianite was discovered, identified and named by Sir Humphrey Davey in the early nineteenth century. By the shores of the loch Kilcamb Lodge Hotel has a particular reputation for gourmet cooking.

Beyond Strontian lies the area of Ben Resipole, a favoured mountain for climbers. Below the mountain on the loch side there is a caravan site and golf course, popular with the caravanning fraternity. Incidentally the golf course has a shop and a club bar open to the public!

The village of **Salen** can be seen from the site, further along the shore. Salen (saline or salty) is mainly known for its production of farmed prawns, most of which are exported to France and Spain.

Through **Glen Borrodale**, with its nineteenth century castle built for the Boots (Chemists) family, through more wild woodland to the Glen Mor Nature Centre, it is not far to **Kilchoan**, a ferry point to Tobermory on the Isle of Mull. The ruin of Mingarry Castle can be seen from the Ferry quay. Kilchoan has a visitor centre, café and is the last village of size before the lighthouse. It is six miles from the point. From the point the only way is back!

The most westerly point on the British mainland, the lighthouse – another creation of the Stevenson brothers – the long journey rewards the effort. The views from the point cover the small isles of Rhum, Eigg, Muck and Canna to the north, Coll to the west, and the Treshnish Isles to the south. At the point there is a tearoom and toilets, and though the lighthouse is no longer manned, there is a small exhibition of the operation of the light, and its history.

Ardnamurchan Point
Ariundle (Cozyknits) 01967 402279
Kilchoan Community Centre 01972 510711
Resipole Farm Campsite(Golf) 019767 431235
Lighthouse 01972 510210

The Isle of Mull

Duart Castle

THE ISLAND of **Mull** has been poetically praised, sung over and generally regarded as one of the most agreeable islands on which to settle. The island has been a Mecca for retired colonial officers over the last two hundred years. The influence of the Gulf Stream, despite its exposed Atlantic seaboard position, ensures a mild climate with temperate winters. The main town is Tobermory, though the main ferry port is **Craignure**. The A849 at Craignure runs right to Tobermory and left to Fionnphort and Iona. In fact the road runs right around the island except for the far North, following the coastline most of the way.

The road passing Ulva's Isle on the west side, B8079, follows Loch Na Keal, where it joins another, the B8035 that comes from the head of Loch Scridain and follows the south side of Loch Na Keal, under the infamous 'Gribun', a lowering cliff of black rock that towers above the road leaking water down its face, and continues on to Salen on the east coast. Within Loch Na Keal are several islets, one of which is Inch Kenneth, famous because Unity Mitford was held there in the house on the island, during the last World War.

The Isle of Mull suffered from the Clearances as did the major part of the Highlands. The country was cleared of people and there is no doubt the whole aspect of the island has changed since 1800.

From Craignure the A849 left passes the two major castles on the island, **Torosay Castle**, famous for its association with Winston Churchill, who as a friend of the family visited regularly to paint and indulge in his bricklaying hobby, and **Duart Castle**, home of the Clan Chieftain of the MacLeans worldwide.

Whilst Torosay is a Victorian building, Duart dates from the thirteenth century and is a stronghold in every sense of the word. Both places can be visited and are open to the public throughout the summer. In addition the gardens of Torosay are open separately to the public. The little light railway that operates from Craignure runs to Torosay and back.

Travelling en route to **Fionnphort** past the two castles is Lochdon, a village alongside the shore, the road follows the shore to a point where it forks, right to Fionnphort, left to Loch Buie. Loch Buie is a sea loch on the Ross of Mull, and the road ends at the beach close to the ruins of

Castle Buie, in the grounds of Buie House. Behind the house are the standing stones on a site of great antiquity. To return, it is necessary to retrace your route back to the main road. At the junction can be seen the memorial erected to Dugald MacPhail, a Gaelic poet, known mainly for his poem 'The Isle of Mull'. The memorial is odd; it is constructed using the stones of MacPhail's house, thus denying his heirs his most valuable asset.

Beyond the castles and the MacPhail memorial the road passes through planted woodland and out into the foothills surrounding Ben Mor, the highest point on Mull. Our road extends round the hillside climbing gently. To the left the land drops away and blends into a glen in the hills across

MacPhail Memorial

the valley bottom. Three lochans (small lochs) stretch along the low land. In the first is the remains of a crannog, a man-made island created in the Iron Age as a defensive fort surrounded by water. The road climbs round the hill and starts to drop into Glen Mor. This Glen is described by Stevenson in his book *Kidnapped*, though it bears little resemblance to Stevenson's glen today. The end of the glen is marked by a balancing rock at the far end, and from there the road curves to the right directly towards Ben Mor.

Loch Scridain opens out on our left and the road curves round past the junction with the B8035, signposted Salen on the right. Following the south side of the loch

Pennyghael Bridge

the narrow twisting road passes through Pennyghael and across the hump backed bridge beside the Pennyghael Hotel. From here there are several miles of twisting road to Bunessan, a small fishing village six miles from Fionnphort, the village from which the ferry to **Iona** runs. The island with the Abbey by the shore is in view the moment you approach the ferry crossing.

St Columba is generally credited with bringing Christianity to the Scotland. He did not. Christianity was here nearly two hundred years before St Columba and on his arrival at Iona he was said to have been greeted by three of the eight Bishops in residence at the time. He did have a great deal of influence in the spread of the Irish rather than Roman Christianity thereafter.

Iona is a tiny island no more than three miles long and perhaps half a mile wide. At the north end there are silver sand beaches, though they are not extensively used. The small settlement at Martyrs Bay contains a restaurant, general store and a minimarket, but it is geared, apart from tourist items, for the tiny population of the island. The ruin of the Nunnery has been consolidated and the

The Abbey, Iona

gardens have been laid out to welcome travellers. On the way to the **Abbey** the road passes the Parish Church, this is one of the forty churches built by Thomas Telford during the construction of the Caledonian Canal.

The Abbey graveyard is said to house the remains of Scottish Kings and Chieftains though none of the graves is actually identified. The last King to be buried here was MacBeth, quite unfairly made infamous by Shakespeare. After MacBeth, kings were buried in Dunfermline. John Smith, the former Labour leader is buried here.

Iona is largely given over to religious matters and it does have a feeling of tranquillity. There are some B&Bs as well as hotels and other accommodation on the island. In the main, accommodation is dedicated to people on retreat and study courses at the now, multifaith Abbey. The ferry only carries cars owned by islanders or delivery vehicles carrying goods for the island.

A purpose-built fishing village from the nineteenth century, **Tobermory** was intended to be a place where such population as remained on the isle of Mull could make a living and help re-populate an island drained of

Tobermory

people during the Clearances. It became the major ferry port for the island, and is the capital of Mull. Although a ferry still operates from Tobermory, it is now only the small ferry to Kilchoan on the Ardnamurchan peninsula. The large ferry, to and from Oban, now only serves Craignure, a considerably shorter journey. The town has declined in importance over the years, the fishing has now been reduced to mainly sport fishing, though scuba diving in and around the area has become popular. The advent of TV has revitalised the area through 'Balamory', a favourite with children. The series has been filmed in Tobermory and the picturesque coloured houses on the harbour front are now a familiar sight to most TV viewers. The coloured houses, so much a feature of the town, must be kept decorated with the same colours. This is apparently a condition of purchase.

Sea Eagle

The Tobermory distillery is the only one on the island and produces both blended and single malt whiskies. Many cruise ships include the town on their itineraries.

During the late twentieth century, Sea Eagles were re-introduced into Mull. The successful project was based on Loch Frisa where the breeding birds can be observed, and at present protected. Since the experiment began, more and more of these magnificent birds have been observed along the west coast. To visit the viewing point it is necessary to make an appointment in advance.

Isle of Mull
Torosay Castle & Gardens 01680 821421
Duart Castle 01680 812309
Tobermoray Distillery 01688 302645
Iona
Martyr's Bay Restaurant 01681 700382

The Isle of Skye

Sgurr nan Gillean

THE ISLE of **Skye** is the largest of the Inner Hebrides and is in fact the second biggest island off the coast of Britain; 48 miles long, its coastline is in excess of 1200 miles of lochs and inlets. The south of the island is largely MacDonald country. The main road runs from the Skye Bridge, north through Broadford to Portree.

From Portree there are two main routes north. First through the town and along the east coast to Staffin, Storr and past the Kilt Rocks and Duntulm Castle to Flodigarry, where Flora MacDonald made her home and is remembered with an imposing statue. Flodigarry has a living museum in the form of a reconstructed village showing the way of life of an earlier time.

This road comes to the town of **Uig**, ferry port for the routes to Loch Maddy on Uist and Tarbert on Harris. Between Uig and the eastern coast lies the Quiraing, a region of strange tortuous rock. There is a road through this area, but not for the faint hearted.

From Uig the road south takes the traveller along the coast of a large sea loch named Loch Snizort. On the other side of the loch is the peninsula that includes **Dunvegan Castle**, home of the Chieftain of the Clan MacLeod, rulers of the north of Skye from the eighth century.

The Talisker distillery is also on the west side of the island though further south and on the other side of yet another sea loch, Loch Harport. From Dunvegan there is a direct road to Portree. However if you wish to continue south the road joins the Portree–Skye Bridge road at Sligachan Bridge, passing the majestic slopes of Sgurr nan Gillean, one of the more famous Cuillins. On the Talisker road there is the Skye Silver visitor centre, with its fine display of craftwork. Tours can be arranged at the distillery for interested visitors.

Broadford is the second largest centre on the island and lies between the bridge and Portree close to the Armadale road. Once an important ferry port, the quay has little use these days and Broadford now services passing visitors to Portree and to Elgol a little village on Loch Scavaig, beyond the mountain Blaven, in the Black Cuillins. Elgol was the home of Lillian Beckwith, the author of many stories of island life. Between Broadford and the Bridge is the airfield on the left, and on the right the road to Kylerhea, the oldest ferry to and from Skye. The ferry is a small one and it is best to check before

Crofters Cottage - Skye

undertaking the serpentine road found at both ends of the crossing. Once undertaken, the scenery is well worth the effort.

The ferry from Mallaig goes to **Armadale**, home of the MacDonald clan chief. Just five minutes walk from the pier, is the Clan Donald centre based on the ruined castle, gardens and museum, focus of the clan worldwide. There is a restaurant and bar within the stables with the ubiquitous gift shop. The museum is a useful source of information for historians.

Following the shores of the Sound of Sleat up to Knock Bay, here can be seen the ruins of Knock Castle, once the haven of piratical MacDonalds, who issued from the shelter of the castle to raid passing merchantmen. The story goes that they attacked a naval ship by mistake, and the castle was destroyed. The few remaining stumps of rock wall are all that remain.

Duisdale House, now a hotel, was once one of the big houses of the island. Significantly the natural vegetation of the area, as at Armadale, was untouched by the

Armadale Castle

Clearances that devastated the way of life including the vegetation elsewhere on the island. Then to Isle Ornsay, with its lighthouse where once Gavin Maxwell lived and studied otters, the view is breathtaking.

At Broadford you can turn right to Kyleakin and Skye Bridge, or left to the north and **Portree**, named Royal Haven, legend has it, by a king passing through the Minch. Caught out by a sudden squall, his ship ran to shelter behind the big bluff that protects the harbour. Finding hospitality from the people living on the shore, it is said

Portree Skye

he named the place Royal Haven or Royal Port (Portrigh in Gaelic). The main centre on the island, Portree has a town square, a main street, several hotels and eating places, beside the harbour. There is also a heritage centre. Outside the harbour can be seen the point of the island of Raasay. There is a backpacker's hostel, and the town is a centre for touring the island by bus, car and cycle, or on foot. The harbour is regularly visited by passing yachts and cruise liners.

The MacLeods were descended from the Viking families who settled on Skye in the eighth century. When the island reverted to Scottish rule after the Battle of Largs in 1263, the MacLeods decided to stay on. It is believed they took the Scottish prefix 'Mac', rather than the Norwegian suffix, 'son' to make it easier to fit into their new environment. Parts of **Dunvegan castle** date from as early as the ninth century though many additions have been made over the years. It became the residence of the MacLeod Chieftain's family in 1200, and has been occupied by the family ever since. It is the home of the 'Fairy Flag', said to have been captured from the Saracens during the Crusades. It is reputed to bring victory to the clan if it is waved during conflict, if spread on the marriage bed it will endow the Chief with children. It was a gift from the fairies on condition it was only used in emergencies. The castle is open to the public during the summer season and is the centre of the MacLeod Clan worldwide.

Dunvegan Castle

Isle of Skye
Talisker Distillery 01478614300
Clan Donald Centre 01471 844305
Skye Silver 01470 511263

Eilean Donan Castle

A CASTLE has stood on St.Donan's Island since around 1200. Built by the Lord of the Isles, it was extended over the years under the stewardship of the MacRae Clan who held the castle on behalf of the Clan MacKenzie. For many years the castle withstood the attacks of man and weather, however in 1719, the castle was in the hands of Spanish Jacobites. It seems they discovered the wine cellars and were incapable of pointing the guns to beat off the attack of the Royal Naval Frigate HMS *Worcester*. The ship pounded the castle to rubble.

The restoration started during the late nineteenth century, but was not completed until 1928, when Colonel MacRae was able to finish the job. In the mid 1930s, the local Priory closed, and the stones from that building were donated to create the causeway that now spans the water between the island and the shore. It now seems to epitomise the Highlands. It certainly is the most photographed castle in Scotland outside Edinburgh.

The Land, the Weather & Midges

TRAVELLERS to the West Highlands are normally warned, by so-called well-wishers, to ensure they bring stout clothing and plenty of insect repellent, to ward off the foul weather and midges. We do get rain and midges, but we also get beautiful

Red squirrel

sunshine and refreshing breezes that keep the midges at bay. No one comes to Scotland to sunbathe, but a surprising number do just that. The beaches here are incredible, great sweeps of golden and silver sand, beside clear seas.

The climate here is like that elsewhere, a mixture of good, bad and indifferent. The constant is the scenery. The sunrises, sunsets, mountain vistas, lochs, burns and waterfalls. On lonely moors, forests and waters can be seen red deer, wild birds and otters. Red squirrels survive here, and can be seen if you know where to look.

The impression that the Highlands of Scotland are covered in huge pine forests, is quite widely accepted. Though there are pine forests, they are of comparatively recent origin. The great plantations of Norwegian and Sitka Spruce were planted to produce a income from areas that had been stripped of trees during the Clearances. The subsequent planting was commercial. The original forests were mainly Oak, Birch, Alder and Rowan, with stands of Scots Pine scattered about the area.

The Musicians

WHEREVER you travel throughout the Highlands, you will encounter the sound of bagpipes. Somehow the combination of wild untamed scenery and the elemental sound of the pipes combine to create an ambience uniquely Scottish. The piper will be dressed traditionally and there is usually a photograph to be taken. The wayside pipers do provide local colour on a journey. Our picture is of Murdo Urquhart, a well known piper who can usually be seen and heard in a lay-by north of **Drumnadrochit** on the Inverness road. It's worth stopping for the music and a photograph, though it can be crowded if a holiday coach has stopped.

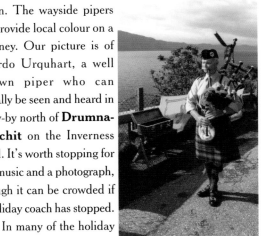

In many of the holiday hotels you can hear fiddle and accordion playing – the standard is generally high. Most schools encourage learning and playing music and the resulting fiddle and pipe bands are well worth hearing. Scottish fiddlers travel the world reminding settlers abroad of their heritage through music.

The Waters

THE WATERS of the Western Highlands are varied and spectacular, the many waterfalls and lochs of fresh water, contrast with the salt water lochs and the coastal waters. Mountains sweeping down to the sea and the loch sides have a beauty all of their own, and lure many of our

visitors to spend time sailing and riding the pleasure craft and ferries.

From Fort William regular trips can be taken to the Seal Island in Loch Linnhe, and there is now a high speed adventure service during the summer months.

Oban provides a combination of all three experiences, with pleasure trips from the Esplanade, and ferries to Mull, and the Outer Hebrides. There is also a small ferry to Lismore.

Our picture shows the *Eye of the Wind* on her return from Bergen, after the Tall Ships Race. Sailing boats can be hired in most places, not forgetting the Caledonian Canal, where cruising boats can be hired to travel the length of the canal and through the three lochs. Facilities can also be found for those bringing their own craft.

Marinas, moorings and servicing centres exist in most loch side resorts and seaside harbours.

Puffer Vic 32

Ferries to Skye and the small isles of Rhum, Eigg, Muck and Canna, can be taken at Mallaig. Another feature of the waters of the Minch is the Puffer that still butts its way round the coast, and sometimes through the Crinan and Caledonian canals. The Vic 32 is the sole surviving steam puffer, still gainfully employed, though now carrying passengers rather than cargo. Used during the filming of *The Vital Spark* for TV, Vic 32 evokes memories of the days when these little craft sailed all around the Scottish coast, servicing the small communities on the outer islands, who often had no other link with the mainland.

Red Kite

The Road to Inverness

THERE ARE alternative routes to Inverness, the best known being the road through **Roy Bridge**.

Turn right off the A82 at the corner past Spean Bridge Woollen Mill and follow the A86 north east through the village of Roy Bridge. As you pass through you will see signposted Glen Roy on the left. The hill above is the site of the last Clan Battle in 1688 between the MacDonnells and the MacIntoshes.

Passing along Glen Spean on the hillside to the right can be seen the line of the old narrow-gauge railway that connected the aluminium plant at Fort William with Loch Treig, the source of the water supply for the Hydro Electric scheme that powered the smelter. (Leaving Fort William the pipelines rising up the hillside on the right are the final stage of the system of loch, tunnel and pipeline that carries the water from Loch Treig to the aluminium plant). The loch is hidden from view of the road, which follows the river at this point. The Glenspean Lodge Hotel, uphill on the left is at the place where the glen begins to open out the hills drop away to the south, and high up on the left can be seen the tiny church and graveyard of St. Cyril (Cille Choirill) made famous for its history dating back to the seventeenth century.

Onward up the glen you come to the Laggan dam where it is possible to stop and trace the story of the fifteen mile tunnel through the Nevis Range of mountains, shown in relief on a plaque in the car park beside the Laggan reservoir. Made of brass the plaque faithfully copies the contours of the surrounding area.

From here the road continues into the region of Strathspey and Badenoch, home of the Clan Macpherson. On the left is the mountain Creag Meagaidh, now a nature reserve, and a little further on, the Loch on the right is Loch Laggan. The road follows the loch side for its full length, passing the entrance to the Nature Reserve on the left, and a little further, on the right, Ardverekie House.

Ardverekie House

Known by millions as Glen Bogle House the Victorian country house on the south side of Loch Laggan, was the star of the series 'Monarch of the Glen'. The BBC series has been shown all over the world and it is a matter of extreme frustration that the house can only be seen from the opposite side of the Loch.

The gatehouse to the estate guards the bridge over the river, and itself is a picturesque, fairy tale building, complete with solitary turret. The road winds through the hills passing a small waterfall on the right at the entrance to Strath Mashie.

Crossing the River Spey at the village of Laggan, it is possible to see the loom of the **Cairn Gorm Mountains** on the right, ahead. The road runs along the flat following the course of the river to the town of **Newtonmore**. One of two towns in the centre of the country, the other being **Kingussie**. Separated by a three mile stretch of road, by tradition the rivalry between the two towns is a legend.

In the present day the rivalry is taken out on the shinty field. The two towns have been sharing honours at the top of the league for many years. Newtonmore has a wide main street, with shops and hotels both sides. On the left is the tourist office which is also an art gallery and café. Newtonmore Crafts combines the functions of all three. In addition the owner David Fallows was the ghost artist for the paintings by Molly, in the series 'Monarch of the Glen', and the shop contains a wealth of memorabilia from the series.

Further along the road on the left is 'Waltzing Waters', as its name implies it's a theatre of fountains, lights and music. As you leave town on the right is a Country Museum, with an open view to the vista of the Cairn Gorm mountains on the other side of the Strath.

Three miles more and you enter Kingussie, capital of the Strathspey/Badenoch region. Another one-street town, but with a main line railway station and another Country Museum. For those in a hurry the A9 link is just on the outskirts of town. I recommend the old A9 that passes under the flyover and follows the railway line along the Strath to **Aviemore**. The road passes an old graveyard on the left and makes it quiet way north through the countryside passing the **Kincraig Wildlife Park**. Beyond the park on a bend stand the ruins of a 'Pilgrims Church'.

The origin is obscure, and the name was chosen because of the low entry and exit doors, requiring the worshipper to enter on his or her knees. There may well be other historic explanations for the ruin.

The road winds onwards past the lovely Loch Alvie on the left, to the town of Aviemore, gateway to the Cairn Gorm ski area a few miles away.

The modern town of Aviemore dates from the early 1930s when Lord Fraser, of department store fame, decided to create an après ski resort on the lines of those he had experienced in Switzerland. From a small community on the Inverness road, he started developing the resort, complete with main line rail station and facilities for year-round sporting activities within a ten mile radius of the town centre. The still growing community is a firm favourite with the younger generation.

From the station it is possible to take the **Strathspey railway** on the steam train, to Boat of Garten and Broomhill. The train runs regularly throughout the summer and can provide a dining car service whilst travelling through the beautiful Strathspey countryside.

There are links to the A9 both before and after the town, but for those enjoying a leisurely drive I suggest following the old road north and taking the left turn to Carrbridge and Inverness just a few miles past Aviemore. The village of **Carrbridge** provides a forest theme park called Landmark, identified by the restored steam engine on the left as you enter the village. Very popular with children, the Park provides woodland walks, an aerial walk, an operating sawmill, and an adventure playground. There is also the visitor centre with restaurant. Through the village there is a picturesque bridge, from which the village is named. The old hump-backed bridge partly ruined dating from 1715 over the River Dunaine was built by the Earl of Seafield for the use of funeral parties en-route to the cemetery at Duthil.

Taking the left fork beyond the bridge brings you back to the A9 and ends this scenic section of the road to Inverness.

The Road to Inverness
Glenspean Lodge Hotel 01397 712223
Newtonmore Crafts 01540 673026
Tomatin Distillery 01808 511234
Strathspey Steam Railway 01479 810725

Carrbridge